HOW CHRISTMAS
SLOTH
BECAME A
CHRISTMAS BOSS

Dedicated to

Addy, Ayden, Coltyn, Aria, Brooklyn,
Isabella, Camilla, Redd, Maddox,
Ezra, Cash, and Makoa!

Hear ye hear ye we proclaim today
Santa has the floor with a nay or a yea

Every year from February to May
Santa picks helpers for Christmas Day

Come all elves to Santa City
Please be ready to make Christmas
morning magical and pretty

You have to be fast and be on your toes
#1 elf record, 3 seconds per wrap with a beautiful bow

One March morning a candidate signed in
The office elf manager couldn't help but grin

Sir are you sure your in the right place?
Slowly smiling it took him forever to plead his case

Ma'am forgive me and if I may
I'm not leaving till I get my way

I am a sloth as you can see
To work for Santa has been a dream for me

I just need a chance to prove my worth
I can do this despite being a sloth since birth

Reluctant and doubtful she gave him a number
All sloth could think was when can I slumber

I'm finally here it took me years to walk
considering the workshop is on the next block

He entered the workshop, all magical and red
So many thoughts were in his sloth head

A big, large man with a belly came in
Oh my stars, it's him, it's him!

Santa hollered bring everyone to me
What new talent do we have? I can't wait to see

Sloth got nervous, he had cold feet
How will I do this, I can't compete

A very kind reindeer shot him a glance
If I recall his name was Dance

Dance took his paw and went around the back way
All of a sudden Santa winked. Dance he's good, he's ok

Santa picked him up on his jolly old lap
Sloth was so excited he took a nap

Hello Sloth, my name is Kris Kringle
Can you hold this hand bell and jingle jingle?

As sloth jingled and his bell echoed out
The other candidates left with a pout

Santa nudged sloth with a loud hohoho!
Welcome to the team sloth, shall we give it a go?

Sloth took an hour and finally said yes
Again he fell asleep on Santa's chest

Sloth was hired, his dream came true
Sloth stayed brave and look what he could do

Elves on the street would wave and smile
Sloth would wave back but it took him awhile

Sloth is the bell boss Santa made known
He's taught young elves about perfect tone

Over the centuries he has hired and taught
Sloth is a Christmas legend, who would have thought

Still each Christmas you'll hear the hand bell ring
And the beautiful spirit of Christmas Sloth and his
his hand bell ringers bring!

Merry Merry Christmas,

Love,

Christmas Sloth and Santa

NOTE

Made in the USA
Las Vegas, NV
18 December 2023